# ASSESSMENT in Cycles of Improvement

★ ★ ★ ★ ★ ★ ★ ★ ★ ★ ★ ★ ★ ★ ★ ★ ★ ★ ★

## Faculty Designs for Essential Learning Outcomes

BY ROSS MILLER

Association of American Colleges and Universities

1818 R Street, NW, Washington, DC 20009

Copyright © 2007 by the Association of American Colleges and Universities. All rights reserved.

ISBN 0-9779210-9-3

To order additional copies of this publication or to find out about other AAC&U publications, visit www.aacu.org, e-mail pub_desk@aacu.org, or call 202.387.3760.

*This publication was made possible by a grant from the Teagle Foundation. The statements made and views expressed are solely the responsibility of the author.*

# Contents

★ ★ ★ ★ ★ ★ ★ ★ ★ ★ ★ ★ ★ ★ ★ ★ ★

PREFACE ................................................................................................................ v

INTRODUCTION ................................................................................................... 1

KNOWLEDGE OF HUMAN CULTURES AND THE PHYSICAL AND NATURAL WORLD

    Mathematical Knowledge and Appreciation: Agnes Scott College ...................... 7

INTELLECTUAL AND PRACTICAL SKILLS

    Quantitative Literacy: Alverno College ................................................................ 9

    Written Communication: Carleton College ....................................................... 11

    Written Communication: Grinnell College ....................................................... 13

    Oral Communication: Case Western Reserve University ................................. 15

    Information Literacy: Earlham College .............................................................. 17

    Inquiry and Critical Thinking: Worcester Polytechnic Institute ....................... 19

    Teamwork and Problem Solving: Portland State University ............................ 21

PERSONAL AND SOCIAL RESPONSIBILITY

    Civic Engagement: Wagner College ................................................................... 23

    Ethical Practice: University of Charleston ........................................................ 25

    Intercultural Knowledge and Competence: Drury University ......................... 27

    Foundation and Skills for Lifelong Learning: San José State University ......... 29

INTEGRATIVE LEARNING

    Integration and Synthesis across General and Specialized Studies: Hampshire College .................... 31

REFERENCES ....................................................................................................... 33

ABOUT THE AUTHOR ....................................................................................... 34

## Liberal Education & America's Promise

★ ★ ★ ★ ★ ★ ★ ★ ★ ★ ★ ★ ★ ★ ★

**Other titles in the series:**

*Liberal Education Outcomes: A Preliminary Report on Student Achievement in College* (2005)

*Communicating Commitment to Liberal Education: A Self-Study Guide for Institutions* (2006)

*Making the Case for Liberal Education: Responding to Challenges,* by Debra Humphreys (2006)

*College Learning for the New Global Century: A Report from the National Leadership Council for Liberal Education and America's Promise* (2007)

For more information about the Liberal Education and America's Promise initiative, visit www.aacu.org/LEAP.

# Preface

★ ★ ★ ★ ★ ★ ★ ★ ★ ★ ★ ★ ★ ★ ★ ★ ★ ★ ★

Liberal Education and America's Promise (LEAP) is a decade-long national initiative launched by the Association of American Colleges and Universities (AAC&U) in 2005 to align the goals for college learning with the needs of the new global century. Extending the work of AAC&U's Greater Expectations initiative, LEAP seeks to engage the public with core questions about what really matters in college, to give students a compass to guide their learning, and to make the aims and outcomes of a liberal education—broad knowledge, intellectual and practical skills, personal and social responsibility, and integrative learning—the accepted framework for excellence at all levels of education. The LEAP initiative is especially concerned with students who, historically, have been underserved in higher education.

LEAP includes three primary and concurrent strands of work:
- A *public advocacy campaign* for liberal education, which is carried out nationally by the educational, business, community, and policy leaders in the LEAP National Leadership Council and regionally through advocacy initiatives in a series of pilot states
- The *Campus Action Network*, which comprises campuses of every kind from across the country that are working with LEAP to articulate high expectations for liberal education and to connect educational practices and assessments to those expectations transparently
- A *research initiative* designed to provide evidence on selected outcomes of a liberal education and periodic public reports on progress in helping students meet twenty-first-century educational standards

LEAP addresses the entire college curriculum, including both professional fields and the liberal arts and sciences. The overarching principles that define liberal education changed fundamentally in the early part of the twentieth century, when the academic disciplines displaced the classical "core" curriculum. In the twenty-first century, the principles of liberal education are again changing. Contemporary liberal education has expanded to foster the deep learning and the practical skills and experience that all students need. It has become more powerful by bridging the traditional divides between "liberal" and "applied" learning in order to prepare students for success in a diverse democracy and an interconnected world.

Through LEAP, AAC&U is working with campuses to accelerate the pace of change and organize campus–community dialogues about the educational issues at stake. At a time when so many are seeking a college education, students deserve far better guidance on the kinds of learning that will serve them best in the era ahead. Highly intentional planning, teaching, and assessment to improve learning and sustain student engagement are needed to ensure that students achieve the sophisticated outcomes expected from a contemporary liberal education.

The LEAP initiative's first publication, *Liberal Education Outcomes: A Preliminary Report on Student Achievement in College* (AAC&U 2005), makes the case for the importance of such an education.

Finding that national, standardized data present a confusing picture of student learning, the authors of *Liberal Education Outcomes* suggest that campuses should focus not on national data but on local efforts in teaching and assessment to improve student learning.

*Assessment in Cycles of Improvement* builds on *Liberal Education Outcomes* by reporting on the efforts of individual campuses to foster student learning in essential outcomes through careful planning, teaching, assessment, and use of data for improvement. It also addresses a major recommendation of the 2007 national LEAP report, *College Learning for the New Global Century*. In that report, the LEAP National Leadership Council argues that assessment can be used "to deepen learning and to establish a culture of shared purpose and continuous improvement," and specifically "recommends that assessments be linked to the essential learning outcomes" and "embedded at milestone points in the curriculum" (AAC&U 2007, 40–41). The campus stories collected in this publication clearly illustrate how institutions can create sequential assessments linked to essential outcomes across the years of a program.

The author wishes to acknowledge the grant support and encouragement of the Teagle Foundation, which made the collecting and writing of the stories possible. Helpful faculty and administrators on each featured campus graciously answered questions and critiqued drafts. These individuals include

- Laura Palucki Blake, James Diedrick, Alan Koch, Myrtle Lewin, Larry Riddle, and James Wiseman at Agnes Scott College;
- Sue Mente at Alverno College;
- Jackie Lauer-Glebov and Carol Rutz at Carleton College;
- Bradley Bateman at Grinnell College;
- Peter Whiting at Case Western Reserve University;
- Tom Kirk at Earlham College;
- Richard Vaz at Worcester Polytechnic Institute;
- Sukhwant Jhaj and Seanna Kerrigan at Portland State University;
- Julia Barchitta at Wagner College;
- Alan Belcher and Karen Merriman at the University of Charleston;
- Richard Schur at Drury University;
- Steven Weisler at Hampshire College.

Shelley Johnson Carey, Michael Ferguson, Darbi Bossman, and all of the staff in AAC&U's Office of Communications and Public Affairs brought creativity and imagination to the planning, editing, and design of this publication. Finally, thanks to those individuals from LEAP Campus Action Network campuses whose stories, sent in response to earlier requests, sparked the effort to create this collection.

# Introduction

Over the last two decades, colleges and universities have increasingly focused on student learning, moving gradually from "teacher-centered" cultures dominated by the traditional lecture toward "learning-centered" priorities. While the idea that college should be about learning may seem obvious, creating a learning-centered culture requires attitudes and actions that have not always been commonplace in higher education. For instance, a learning-centered campus
- holds expectations for all students to achieve at high levels;
- creates clear goals for learning and provides appropriate and sufficient experiences to ensure that students reliably reach the goals;
- provides resources to engage and coach students having difficulties;
- uses data from assessments, both formative and summative, to improve learning and teaching.

Put another way, a learning-centered campus strives for more effective levels of learning based upon clear goals, aligned experiences, multiple assessments, and improvements suggested by data from assessment. Learning suffers when any part of this cycle is neglected: students who might have otherwise succeeded may fail as a result.

At many campuses, the most difficult (and sometimes contentious) part of the cycle is assessment. Policy leaders have gradually increased their demands for assessment, asking institutions to establish clear goals for learning and provide evidence to confirm that learning goals are being reached. These demands for evidence of learning have led to requests for data at the course and individual student levels that can be aggregated for program and institutional purposes. But since many professors have been taught neither how to teach nor how to develop valid and reliable assessments, it is no surprise that faculty struggle to meet the demands of accreditors or administrators seeking data on student learning. While most teachers have a good idea of how well their students are doing, the process of creating analytical judgments of student work, of inventing language and rubrics to explain the complex outcomes of sophisticated learning, presents a major challenge—one that many have resisted and others claim is infeasible.

Much progress is being made, however. Increased attention to learning and assessment has resulted in innovative practices like scoring complex learning with rubrics, teaching students to self-assess, and using student portfolios to provide evidence of learning. The belief that assessment data must be *quantitative* is gradually fading on campuses. Once learning goes beyond the most basic levels, meaningful assessment nearly always requires *qualitative* judgments of the elements vital to authentic work in a domain. In fact, much of the resistance to assessment of student learning over the last two decades derives from a narrow view of assessment as an attempt to "measure" learning quantitatively. A common objection is "you can't put a number on what my students do."

Faculty are finding that valid and reliable information about learning can be gleaned from purposeful, qualitative assessments ranging from short course assignments to yearlong projects, public oral presentations, and observations of internships and other off-campus placements. Such data are vital to improving individuals' learning and are also central to course-level improvements.

The shift toward qualitative data, however, puts campuses at odds with many policy makers' assumptions about assessment, which frequently emphasize comparable, standardized tests. Yet, as assessment experts themselves will point out (Shavelson 2007), there are no standardized measures—much less sophisticated, high-level measures—for most of the outcomes of a twenty-first-century liberal education. Thus it is all the more important for faculty members to turn a spotlight on curriculum-embedded practices that are effective not just at documenting the level of learning, but also at raising it.

In the final analysis, if data appropriate to specific purposes are gathered, both quantitative and qualitative assessments will be important to a campus's assessment plan. Examples of this are present in the stories in this collection.

The purpose of this monograph is to share campus stories of highly intentional approaches to learning that (1) begin with clear goals for learning, (2) move to logically related learning experiences, (3) include assessments to monitor the quality of learning, and (4) foster improvements based upon assessment data. Common practice often fails to utilize all facets of this ideal teaching/learning cycle. While course syllabi may include learning goals and a series of learning experiences (readings, papers, projects, presentations, etc.), assessment that validly and reliably reveals individual student achievement is *often* neglected. Using assessment data for revisions and improvement is *very often* neglected. Data that are intentionally collected and then interpreted by faculty and departments have the potential to systematically improve teaching and learning. The stories that follow illustrate how individual campuses are working to make such improvements for a wide range of liberal education outcomes.

## Essential Liberal Education Outcomes

The Greater Expectations initiative, which was launched by the Association of American Colleges and Universities (AAC&U) in 2000 and concluded in 2006, convened a national panel of K–12, business, community, and higher education leaders to formulate a statement of the aims and purposes of higher education in the twenty-first century (AAC&U 2002). The initiative also drew upon conversations across hundreds of college and university campuses about important outcomes and the practices used to achieve them. At the same time, AAC&U's Project on Accreditation and Assessment brought together regional and specialized accreditors to discuss the outcomes important to all college students, regardless of major or professional emphasis (AAC&U 2004b). The work of these groups affirmed that in the twenty-first century, all citizens need the learning outcomes traditionally associated with a liberal education.

Drawing directly from this earlier work, AAC&U's Liberal Education and America's Promise (LEAP) initiative has defined a set of educational outcomes that all students need from higher learning, outcomes that are closely aligned with the challenges of a complex and volatile world (AAC&U 2004b, 2007). Keyed to work, life, and citizenship, the essential learning outcomes of a contemporary liberal education should be fostered across general education and the majors, including professional studies. They provide a new framework to guide students' cumulative progress—as well as curricular alignment—from school through college. The chart on page 3

# *The Essential Learning Outcomes*

Beginning in school, and continuing at successively higher levels across their college studies, students should prepare for twenty-first-century challenges by gaining:

### ★ Knowledge of Human Cultures and the Physical and Natural World

- Through study in the sciences and mathematics, social sciences, humanities, histories, languages, and the arts

**Focused** *by engagement with big questions, both contemporary and enduring*

### ★ Intellectual and Practical Skills, including

- Inquiry and analysis
- Critical and creative thinking
- Written and oral communication
- Quantitative literacy
- Information literacy
- Teamwork and problem solving

**Practiced extensively**, *across the curriculum, in the context of progressively more challenging problems, projects, and standards for performance*

### ★ Personal and Social Responsibility, including

- Civic knowledge and engagement—local and global
- Intercultural knowledge and competence
- Ethical reasoning and action
- Foundations and skills for lifelong learning

**Anchored** *through active involvement with diverse communities and real-world challenges*

### ★ Integrative Learning, including

- Synthesis and advanced accomplishment across general and specialized studies

**Demonstrated** *through the application of knowledge, skills, and responsibilities to new settings and complex problems*

**Note:** This listing was published originally in *College Learning for the New Global Century* (AAC&U 2007). The findings summarized here are also documented in previous publications of the Association of American Colleges and Universities: *Greater Expectations: A New Vision for Learning as a Nation Goes to College* (2002), *Taking Responsibility for Quality of the Baccalaureate Degree* (2004), and *Liberal Education Outcomes: A Preliminary Report on Achievement in College* (2005).

describes the outcomes and organizes them into the areas of knowledge, intellectual and practical skills, personal and social responsibility, and integrative learning.

To foster these essential outcomes, campuses are using a range of pedagogical practices and curricular arrangements shown through research to be effective: first-year seminars and experiences, common intellectual experiences, learning communities, writing-intensive courses, collaborative assignments and projects, undergraduate research of many kinds, intercultural and global experiences, service learning, community-based learning, internships, and capstone courses and projects.

## Campus Stories

Each story that follows tells about the achievement of one or more of these liberal education outcomes. Early in the planning of this publication, a decision was made not to try to cover the dozens of possible areas of knowledge: knowledge has long been a top priority within the academy, with resources and planning focused on its acquisition. Intentional development of intellectual and practical skills, personal and social responsibility, and integration are much less understood and, consequently, are the primary focus of these stories. However, it is important to emphasize that liberal education outcomes develop through the application of knowledge in disciplinary, interdisciplinary, and multidisciplinary contexts. Thus, the inclusion of only one story about knowledge (mathematical knowledge and appreciation at Agnes Scott College) should not be interpreted as deemphasizing knowledge. Knowledge acquisition is a key liberal education outcome and is the foundation for all other outcomes.

The format of the stories reflects the structure of the teaching/learning cycle mentioned above—setting goals, fostering achievement of the goals, assessing the outcomes, and making improvements based on assessment data. In several cases, the institution's written goals do not cite the exact outcome of the story's title. This circumstance can occur when a campus simply chooses a different term for an outcome than the one AAC&U has chosen or when a campus adopts broad goal areas that subsume several outcomes. Moreover, a robust educational approach (such as independent project work) may foster several different outcomes simultaneously. For example, the stories about inquiry and critical thinking at Worcester Polytechnic Institute and integration and synthesis at Hampshire College both describe practices that foster inquiry and critical thinking as well as integration and synthesis (and undoubtedly other outcomes). For this collection, only a single outcome is discussed even when the institutions themselves mention more than one outcome.

Of course, campuses define their learning outcomes in ways specific to their histories, cultures, and expectations. Regardless of the written definition that anyone may create for a particular outcome, in the end, the outcome is actually defined by what is accepted as evidence that it has been achieved. It may prove easier to begin planning by asking, what does outcome X look like when someone does it well? than to try to write a definition of the outcome. Faculty discussions about how well a particular piece of student work represents what an institution or a department expects for a particular outcome can help shape written definitions and develop campus standards. Shared definitions and standards, in turn, make valid and reliable assessment possible.

The campuses' approaches to achieving outcomes range from highly intentional versions of expected practice to unique responses based on local resources. The point of these stories is not simply to present practices that other campuses can imitate, but also to trigger discussions that lead to creative solutions for the development, assessment, and improvement of student learning on individual campuses. One can begin a discussion by considering how another campus achieves a given outcome and continue by asking, Does our campus value this outcome, and if so, how can we learn from this example as we seek to meet our program and institutional goals?

The stories included in this collection illustrate how outcomes can be developed *over time*. College-level competence in liberal education outcomes rarely develops from a single exposure to learning or through a single course. These sophisticated outcomes require repeated learning experiences and authentic application as they develop over an extended period of time to result in high levels of achievement. In *Our Students' Best Work* (2004a) and in *College Learning for the New Global Century* (2007), AAC&U recommends that institutions use incoming, milestone, and capstone assessments to develop outcomes, to gather evidence, and to provide feedback on student learning throughout a degree program. Many of the campuses chosen for this collection offer multiple opportunities to learn and multiple assessments of the given outcome.

The stories are based on material (such as goals and outcomes, terms and phrases) created by the individual institutions, submitted by individuals on the campuses for inclusion in the stories, and found on institutional Web sites. The author worked with individuals on each of the featured campuses to gather information and shape stories that, to the extent possible given their brevity, are accurate representations of campus practice at the time of writing. Specific sources for information in the stories have not been cited due to the informality of these individuals' correspondence with the author and the transience of Web site content. The author acknowledges that much of the information and language in the stories has been provided by individual campuses and then arranged into a common format.

The campuses featured in the following pages have exerted intentional efforts to improve student learning. Knowledge, skills, time, energy, and creativity are all necessary to the improvement process. But unless administrators, faculty, and staff believe that they *should* work intentionally for improvement and act to make it happen, change efforts will have neither heart nor legs.

Belief and action are evident both in these stories and in the dozens of others that AAC&U staff members hear during campus visits, meetings, and institutes. Our hope is that these stories will contribute to a commitment within higher education to fostering high levels of learning for all students and that they will prompt campuses to take action to that end.

**Knowledge of Human Cultures and the Physical and Natural World**

# Mathematical Knowledge and Appreciation

## AGNES SCOTT COLLEGE (Decatur, Georgia)

### Goals

Agnes Scott College, a women's liberal arts institution, encourages students to pursue mathematics as a discipline while also striving to ensure that each graduate, no matter what her major, has had a positive learning experience in a mathematics course and has developed an understanding of the importance of mathematics within the context of a liberal arts education. This is reflected in the mathematics department's stated mission of helping students "learn to think clearly and logically, to analyze problems, to understand and be able to use the language, theory, and techniques of mathematics, and to develop the skills and acquire the mathematical tools needed in the application of mathematics."

In delineating its goals, the department takes into account three fairly distinct groups of students: mathematics majors intending to pursue graduate study, students pursuing mathematics-related majors or careers (including those intending to teach mathematics), and students intending to take only one required mathematics distribution course. The department has identified broad goals for each of these groups as well as "intended outcomes" that further specify the learning that will occur as part of each broad goal. For example, the department lists the following outcomes under the goal of providing "courses and experiences that will enable students with an interest in mathematics to prepare for a mathematics-related career, including the teaching of mathematics":

- Students will exhibit proficiency in the computational techniques of calculus and linear algebra.
- Students will develop skills in problem analysis and problem solving, both individually and collaboratively.
- Students will be able to use mathematics as a tool for the solution of real-world problems.

The department intends that courses used for the single distribution requirement will "provide both the supportive and enabling atmosphere that would encourage a student to venture into more mathematics when that course is over, and the opportunities for a student to feel that studying more mathematics is in her best interest."

### Fostering Achievement of the Goals

Collaboration is encouraged—when appropriate, students work together on problem sets or independent projects. These projects sometimes involve the application of mathematical skills and knowledge to practical problems. For example, students in a differential equations course may examine issues such as which vaccinations children should be given and when, or what restrictions should be placed on carbon dioxide emissions. These collaborative projects encourage application of and engagement with mathematics across disciplines.

The mathematics department also encourages students to take advantage of tutoring possibilities. The mathematics learning support center provides an environment where conversations about mathematics are expected and encouraged. As a result, the mathematics department continues to develop and maintain a culture where it is natural for students to support and engage one another.

### Assessing the Outcome

The department uses a variety of standardized, local, direct, and indirect assessments to measure student achievement in mathematics.

In every mathematics course, student surveys provide an indirect assessment of learning. The department later disaggregates the results of these surveys in light of course and departmental goals.

The department also analyzes retention figures for introductory mathematics courses to determine the extent to which students drop courses and why they do so. It seeks specifically to address the "math phobia" that some students might have developed prior to college. This is particularly important for students in the Woodruff Scholars Program, which supports nontraditional-age students whose prior experience in mathematics courses may have been disabling or have taken place decades earlier. The retention study, in part, analyzes student confidence based on measures of enrollment and persistence in mathematics courses.

Selected mathematics courses use locally developed, computer-based assessments of calculus skills (differentiation proficiency, integration proficiency, and the ability to solve differential equations). Students pass when they answer all questions correctly. Multiple attempts on different versions of the tests are allowed.

Students majoring in mathematics, math-economics, and math-physics take the Educational Testing Service (ETS) Major Field Test in mathematics during their senior year. The department has established expectations for average percentile scores using the most recent four years of testing to account for fluctuation in the number of majors from year to year.

The capstone seminar for mathematics majors is problem-based, emphasizing students' abilities to ask and solve mathematical questions, pose conjectures, and use mathematical language effectively in both writing and speaking. To find solutions to the problems, students must go beyond the straightforward application of standard techniques, be creative, and synthesize mathematical methods.

### Improvements Resulting from Assessment Data

The assessment process has affected the mathematics curriculum in important ways. For example, lower than anticipated scores for mathematics majors in the past on the "non-routine problem" section of the ETS exam resulted in an increased effort by mathematics faculty to embed non-routine problems in mathematics courses. The senior capstone seminar emphasizes this area as well.

The mathematics department also reaches out to other math-intensive disciplines. A partnership between the mathematics and chemistry departments seeks to offer more structured support for students who are taking introductory chemistry with interlinked support for those also enrolled in beginning calculus. This enables evaluation of how interaction with peer learning assistants and mathematics and chemistry faculty increases students' comfort levels in mathematics and science and the likelihood that they will major in those fields.

# Intellectual and Practical Skills

# Quantitative Literacy

## ALVERNO COLLEGE (Milwaukee, Wisconsin)

### Goals

Alverno College, a liberal arts college for women, requires that all students demonstrate quantitative literacy through the intermediate level over the course of their studies in general education and the major. The college provides the following definitions of different levels of quantitative literacy:
- Beginning level: Interprets mathematics models such as formulas, graphs, and tables and draws reasonable inferences from them
- Intermediate level: Thinks critically about her own and others' use of quantitative information and language
- Advanced level: Integrates quantitative abilities to effectively communicate information and respond to problems within a discipline-related context

Faculty have developed detailed criteria to assess student achievement at each of these levels. At the prerequisite and beginning levels, faculty assess student knowledge and ability in general education quantitative literacy courses. At the intermediate level, assessments focus on quantitative literacy in disciplinary contexts across the curriculum. Faculty (and on occasion other experts) assess advanced quantitative literacy in the context of the major as appropriate to the disciplinary or professional area of study.

### Fostering Achievement of the Goals

Students demonstrate beginning-level quantitative literacy through a general education course, Mathematical Connections. In this course, students gather and organize data, and then use their knowledge of numerical and graphical representations of information to complete a write-up or presentation supporting a particular perspective on their topic. The course covers probability by exploring why counting concepts are important to citizens—students consider, in particular, the design of personal identifiers such as phone numbers, social security numbers, and license plates. Similarly, when students study measurement concepts, they discuss measurements needed for communication in science and medicine. They also explore topics like the geometric advantage of a cylindrical soda can. Students often take other general education courses that support their quantitative literacy development while they are enrolled in Mathematical Connections. When teachers of Mathematical Connections make direct reference to other contexts that require quantitative literacy, and when teachers of the other general education courses make reference to the quantitative literacy course, students learn to apply their abilities in different settings.

Students must demonstrate intermediate-level quantitative literacy within a discipline-based course. Each major course sequence includes multiple opportunities for students to develop and demonstrate quantitative literacy. This graduation requirement helps to promote "quantitative literacy across the curriculum" in a way reminiscent of the long-established "writing across the curriculum" process.

Alverno College's unique approach helps students realize the important role of quantitative literacy in their particular area of study. It is not an add-on but an integral part of the discipline. Each course emphasizes areas of quantitative literacy that are most pertinent to the discipline and to students' intended professions. For example, as English majors study form and structure in literature, they analyze text in terms of symmetry and proportion and then create geometric models to represent their analyses. In studying two poems about Harlem, one from the 1940s and one more contemporary, students might also analyze government data related to how Harlem and its residents have changed over time. Students in a history class, in looking at women's roles in governments both ancient and modern, may analyze qualitative and quantitative data, make estimations and extrapolate where data are missing, and deduce trends over long periods of time. In these and other ways, major areas contribute intentionally to the development of quantitative literacy.

### Assessing the Outcome

Faculty assess students' beginning-level abilities using common assessments across all sections of the general education quantitative literacy course. Faculty meet to ensure a consistent level of expectation across the course.

Within the discipline-based courses, the college's intermediate-level quantitative literacy criteria are used for assessment. Students demonstrate quantitative literacy through assessments integrated into the courses. The college quantitative literacy subgroup serves as a resource for faculty and as an oversight group to ensure a consistent level of expectation across the college.

Advanced-level quantitative literacy is integrated into the outcomes of majors as appropriate. At this level, quanitative literacy criteria are completely absorbed into the criteria of these majors.

### Improvements Resulting from Assessment Data

Data from assessments have driven changes in the teaching and assessment of quantitative literacy in the general education and discipline-based courses. At the general education level, teachers found that students were not able to demonstrate adequate depth of quantitative literacy in novel situations. As a result, the college expanded the number of contact hours for the course to allow teachers to provide students with extended opportunities to explore a wider range of applications of quantitative literacy criteria. At the intermediate level, teachers found that students were not appreciating the integral role of quantitative literacy within their disciplines because some faculty were teaching and assessing in a way that made quantitative literacy separate from the other content of their courses. After realizing that this approach was counterproductive, teachers worked to infuse quantitative literacy seamlessly into their activities and assessments so that students could better demonstrate understanding of quantitative literacy as it applies to the disciplines.

# Intellectual and Practical Skills

# Written Communication

## CARLETON COLLEGE (Northfield, Minnesota)

### Goals

Carleton College uses a sophomore writing portfolio to ensure that students are ready to write well as they progress in their majors. Writing goals and outcomes are identical, defined operationally by the specific kinds of writing required for the portfolio. Students compile the writing portfolio after their third term (at the end of the first year) and no later than the seventh week of the sixth term (at the end of the second year).

The portfolio consists of three to five papers (totaling between ten and thirty double-spaced pages) written for Carleton courses and must include

- papers from at least two of the four curricular divisions (arts and literature, humanities, social sciences, mathematics, and natural sciences);
- at least one paper from a writing-rich course (except for students exempted from the writing-rich course);
- at least one paper that reports on something observed (for example, field notes for geology or sociology, a laboratory report, or a description of art or music);
- at least one paper that demonstrates ability to analyze complex information;
- at least one paper that provides interpretation (of data, a text, a performance, etc.);
- at least one paper that demonstrates ability to identify and effectively use appropriate outside sources, properly documented;
- at least one paper that shows ability to articulate and support a thesis-driven argument.

Some papers will exhibit several of these characteristics, and all papers must demonstrate evidence of effective control of standard American English. Students introduce the portfolio with a reflective paper that details the ways in which the portfolio represents their work and the criteria listed above.

### Fostering Achievement of the Goals

Carleton students are required to pass a writing-rich course with a grade of C- or better. (Students entering with Advanced Placement scores of 5 or International Baccalaureate scores of 7 on English language or literature exams are not required to take a writing-rich course but must still submit a portfolio.) Writing is widely infused throughout courses at Carleton so that most students will have repeated writing experiences in the terms prior to portfolio submission. Since all papers in the portfolio will have previously been graded by Carleton faculty, students will have already received feedback on the quality of work included in the portfolio.

## Assessing the Outcome

Carleton faculty and staff review the portfolios during summer scoring sessions. The faculty and staff members who review portfolios have a wide range of experience and come from different disciplines and programs.

Portfolios are rated as exemplary, passing, or in need of more work. Typically, a very large number of portfolios receive "passing" scores and very few receive ratings of "exemplary" or "needs work." Students whose portfolios are designated "needs work" receive individual counseling from the writing program director and submit additional or revised work to earn a "pass" and satisfy the graduation requirement. The campus celebrates exemplary scores in a public ceremony.

The scoring process is carefully monitored to ensure reliability among scorers each summer and also from year to year. Second readers review all portfolios scored "exemplary" or "needs work," as well as a random sample of "passes." Portfolios from previous years are included in the process as a further check on the reliability of the scoring process.

The scoring process introduces young faculty to campus-wide standards in writing and to the interesting writing assignments that experienced faculty use successfully with students. Data from several years of scoring indicate that the quality of writing required to receive an "exemplary" score is now higher than in the past. In short, the group process of scoring student writing portfolios raises campus expectations for writing among both students and faculty—an interesting unintended consequence of the sophomore writing portfolio.

## Improvements Resulting from Assessment Data

The portfolio process has contributed to an improvement in students' writing abilities. A transcript analysis revealed that students who received "needs work" scores tended to enter Carleton with large gaps between their high SAT mathematics scores and their lower SAT verbal scores. Advising these students to take a writing-rich course in their first term on campus has proven to be an effective intervention.

The portfolio process has also triggered curriculum development focused upon writing in the majors. The redesign of senior comprehensive exam protocols and departmental reviews of the use of writing in the major's curriculum have moved the college's emphasis on writing beyond the portfolio and into the majors.

Carleton is now beginning to explore the use of the writing portfolios to assess other parts of the curriculum—for example, by looking at the use of quantitative information in selected assignments that appear in the portfolios. The college discovered that 45 percent of all courses taught at Carleton are represented among the writing products that appear in the portfolios, providing a portal through which to assess several learning outcomes across a large part of the curriculum.

# Intellectual and Practical Skills

# Written Communication

## GRINNELL COLLEGE (Grinnell, Iowa)

### Goals

The undergraduate program at Grinnell College has only one required course—the First-Year Tutorial. Students are responsible for planning their own academic program in conversation with an adviser. An institutional statement of broad goals for education in the liberal arts informs the advising process and guides student choices in both general study and the major.

Grinnell expects students to develop strong communication capabilities. As the college's catalog states,

> Nothing enhances the expression of knowledge better than engaging, clear, and accurate language. Reading closely, thinking clearly, and writing effectively form a web of connected skills, whether practiced in the First-Year Tutorial, in the Writing Lab, in designated writing courses, or in courses ranging from the introductory to the advanced level in almost every discipline. Students planning their academic programs should strive for the ability to convey their ideas with power and grace, to analyze and formulate arguments, and to adapt each piece of writing to its context and audience.

### Fostering Achievement of the Goals

Grinnell College develops students' writing skills through a "writing across the curriculum" approach. Students can choose from among approximately 150 writing-intensive courses each semester.

Beyond these courses, the writing lab at Grinnell helps students improve their writing and achieve individual writing goals, whether academic, professional, or personal. The lab also offers a course—College Writing 100—that students may take twice during their studies at Grinnell. This course serves students especially well in a semester in which they write many papers or complete a long-term writing project, since it provides regular appointments with a writing instructor of the student's choice. Students sign a learning contract at the beginning of the semester, set their own goals for improvement, and evaluate their writing skills at the beginning and end of the semester.

When requested, the writing lab faculty will visit classes to make presentations on selected topics in writing. From explaining criteria for good writing and describing typical assignments that students may encounter to helping students improve sentences, paragraphs, and arguments, these faculty provide valuable assistance.

### Assessing the Outcome

The college monitors students' learning by assessing samples of writing during the first, fourth, and seventh semesters. Faculty teaching a writing-intensive course collect data on the quality of the writing that randomly selected students have completed during the course. The college uses a common rubric consisting of ten elements (each scored on a scale of 1 to 4) to assess the writing samples, and stores the data online to facilitate timely analysis. The rubric itself emerged from faculty discussions and workshops on writing.

The college's Writing Advisory Committee creates formal reports from each fourth- and seventh-semester assessment. The entire faculty discusses the reports in a regular faculty meeting each year. The assessment results also help shape the college's weeklong summer writing workshops, which focus on improving student writing and designing writing assignments for courses.

All new students take the First-Year Tutorial, and during the first six weeks of the first semester, every tutorial teacher assesses the writing of each of his or her students. Grinnell assesses approximately 100 to 125 fourth- and seventh-semester students from among those enrolled in writing-intensive courses. The college has gotten response rates of above 80 percent to the survey request in each of the three semesters. The sample size is large enough to provide good data, but does not overburden individual faculty members.

### Improvements Resulting from Assessment Data

The assessment approach is relatively new: Grinnell conducted the seventh-semester writing assessment for the first time in the 2006–7 academic year. Nevertheless, the data gathered so far in first- and fourth-semester assessments are contributing to improvements in how students support their arguments and order the ideas in their arguments. The process is also helping build faculty understanding and commitment to their "across the curriculum" responsibilities to foster students' writing skills.

# Oral Communication

## CASE WESTERN RESERVE UNIVERSITY (Cleveland, Ohio)

### Goals

A sequence of four seminars (First Seminar, two University Seminars, and a departmental seminar) and a senior capstone project contribute to the development of oral communication skills across all undergraduate degree programs in Case Western Reserve University's Seminar Approach to General Education and Scholarship (SAGES) program. Students choose the interdisciplinary First Seminar and University Seminars from offerings on a wide range of topics related to the social world, the symbolic world, and the natural or technological world. In addition, First Seminar includes a "fourth hour" in which students explore Cleveland's rich cultural resources. Whatever the topic, the development of communication skills is at the heart of the seminar experience.

At the end of First Seminar, students should be able to
- engage in thoughtful, productive discussion with peers, faculty, and other professionals;
- give and receive criticism respectfully and constructively;
- establish a personal voice in oral and written expression;
- present concepts and beliefs in clear, precise, and graceful language;
- frame substantial arguments, first by making interesting claims and then by marshaling and interpreting relevant evidence;
- recognize their responsibilities—as writers and speakers, readers and listeners—in promoting scholarly dialogue, and then meet those responsibilities.

After subsequent seminars, students should be able to
- articulate a question or problem appropriate to the discipline;
- provide useful, relevant criticism to others—and respond constructively to criticism—within a disciplinary context;
- articulate a problem or question that is both interesting and relevant to their chosen field(s) of study;
- produce a substantial presentation in response to a question or problem.

The goals for written and oral communication in SAGES seminars often overlap.

### Fostering Achievement of the Goals

The SAGES program began a three-year pilot phase in 2002; now, it is the general education curriculum for all Case undergraduates. Not just a first-year seminar program, SAGES extends across the entire undergraduate experience. Thus, it offers a unique approach to the development of students' communication skills—both written and oral.

The seminar format, with an enrollment limit of seventeen students, creates a setting in which students participate actively in their learning through discussions, presentations, research, and collaboration. All seminars are writing-intensive and feature both formal and informal work in oral communication. Students also explore modes of inquiry and develop oral communication skills through ongoing class discussions and formal presentations. A faculty member may invite a student to follow up written comments from an online discussion with spoken comments, particularly if the student has not contributed recently to class discussion.

In the two University Seminars and the departmental seminar, students continue to engage in a variety of modes of thinking, writing, and speaking. They develop their skills in effective inquiry, argument, analysis, criticism, and presentation, first across disciplines and finally within a discipline. The senior capstone project culminates in a public oral presentation of a student's independent research or scholarship. In this way, Case builds a culture of communication across the entire undergraduate degree program, providing students many opportunities to improve their oral communication skills.

### Assessing the Outcome

All seminars are assessed with standard university course evaluations and a questionnaire specifically designed to address the goals of SAGES. Faculty responses to questions about seminar outcomes provide program assessment data that can be compared to student responses about seminar outcomes to investigate whether faculty assessments and student perceptions align. Faculty-developed rubrics generate both faculty and peer feedback for formal oral presentations. Redirecting or praising student comments, both in class and during private conferences, are common formative practices used to help shape students' oral communication skills.

Data gathered through the National Survey of Student Engagement during the SAGES pilot phase showed that students who participated in SAGES were statistically more likely to agree that their experience at Case contributed in a substantial manner to their ability to speak clearly and effectively. Similarly, SAGES students were more likely to have made a presentation in class and to have participated in class discussions. The SAGES questionnaires, while administered only in the seminars, documented progress in student perceptions of their oral presentation and discussion skills and allowed Case to learn more about how particular seminar leaders develop these skills.

### Improvements Resulting from Assessment Data

During the program's pilot phase, the SAGES Learning and Research Team visited seminars and talked extensively with faculty and students about their experiences. The team combined the best practices discovered in the pilot courses with current research on teaching and learning to produce a SAGES instructor's guide. The guide reviews the SAGES program's mission and contains seven "modules" on topics ranging from seminar design to fostering critical and ethical thinking among students. A module on group dynamics suggests many ways to encourage discussions and thus improve oral communication. The guide is meant to be a "living document," changing and growing as the SAGES program continues to evolve.

Student and faculty feedback have also resulted in more clearly stated seminar outcomes. Seminar leaders base decisions on how to reach goals on data and a growing body of effective practice.

# Information Literacy

## EARLHAM COLLEGE (Richmond, Indiana)

### Goals

The general education program at Earlham College identifies several goals related to information literacy, including

- the ability to gather information from print and electronic sources and critical capacity to evaluate the data gathered and the ideas encountered;
- close and critical reading, thoughtful reflection, ready discussion, and cogent writing;
- increased adeptness in thoughtfully considering texts of all sorts, whether singly or in comparison with one another.

Information literacy competency standards for higher education influence planning and teaching efforts, and attention is given to information literacy abilities most relevant to a faculty member's proposed assignments or projects (these standards are available from the Association of College and Research Libraries at www.ala.org/ala/acrl/acrlstandards/informationliteracycompetency.htm).

Earlham has a well-established culture of collaboration between librarians and teaching faculty, with librarians directly assisting faculty in planning information-intensive research assignments and projects. Thus, in addition to assisting with *student learning*, the librarians advance *faculty learning* as they help faculty better understand and utilize the library services and resources needed for course assignments.

### Fostering Achievement of the Goals

Faculty make decisions about the delivery of information literacy instruction by considering what is relevant to a particular assignment, project, or course and the previous experiences of students in the class. Librarians contact faculty, particularly newer faculty, to talk about plans for research assignments. Librarians will suggest ways to improve information access and usage, and will also provide guidance on how to teach students to conduct research. Librarians often will teach classes within a course to foster the skills students need for the upcoming assignments. Library facilities and some classrooms allow for group instruction in the use of information and references. One serendipitous outcome of direct librarian contact with students is the increased willingness of students to ask for help while in the library.

Development of information literacy for students begins in the required first-year seminar, a topic-based course in which students read extensively and complete research activities. Another first-year course, Interpretive Practices, focuses on critical thinking, writing, and the use of ideas from multiple sources—intellectual skills needed at many times during college, including when searching for, selecting, and evaluating information. Lower-division general education and elective courses will often include assignments that require further instruction for the skilled use of information and associated technology.

Librarians now assume that the first-year seminar and the Interpretive Practices course have laid a foundation for information literacy, and in advanced courses they work with students to develop a discipline-based approach to research. At the junior and senior levels, as students work intensively in their major courses, the focus of the librarians' work shifts toward teaching students how to access the scholarly literature of the discipline. Students learn about the major sources and journals that provide high-quality information and research results.

The work of the librarians and other faculty is closely intertwined across the undergraduate years so that student learning needs are accommodated efficiently and appropriately. Earlham has built a culture that supports connections between the classroom and the library to ensure improved use of resources and enhanced student learning.

## Assessing the Outcome

Information literacy is assessed through course-embedded assignments. The assessments, which often contribute to a final grade for a paper or project, inform students of their progress toward information literacy goals. Librarians also have conversations with course faculty in which they review how research assignments have worked and try to identify points where the design of the assignment and the instruction can be improved. Because they are involved in both pre-course planning and post-course assessment, librarians are able to gather detailed data about how information literacy is being developed across the undergraduate years and among various programs on campus. This allows them to refine their efforts with students and faculty and gives direction to efforts to refine goals, instruction, and services.

Campus surveys have shown that Earlham students have many experiences in information literacy across their programs. From among the thirty-odd courses that students take in their degree programs, a dozen or more typically include library instruction to assist with research.

## Improvements Resulting from Assessment Data

Assessment of student work has motivated faculty to teach students to go beyond simplistic Internet searches and sources. It has also led them to modify the requirements of assignments to alert students to specific expectations for research. The collaboration between librarians and faculty on assessment has contributed to faculty-initiated changes in course assignments.

As information technology and electronic resources have improved, librarians have changed the way they think about and teach the research process. Instead of providing students with search procedures or focusing on technique, instruction now targets the evaluation of information sources and an iterative process of research, analysis, and framing new questions. In this process, the focus is on identifying what type of resource is most likely to provide the information needed.

# Intellectual and Practical Skills

# Inquiry and Critical Thinking

## WORCESTER POLYTECHNIC INSTITUTE (Worcester, Massachusetts)

### Goals

Worcester Polytechnic Institute (WPI) identifies several undergraduate learning outcomes that are strongly related to inquiry and critical thinking. WPI expects its graduates to
- be able to identify, analyze, and solve problems creatively through sustained critical investigation;
- be able to make connections between disciplines and to integrate information from multiple sources;
- be aware of how their decisions affect and are affected by other individuals separated by time, space, and culture;
- be aware of personal, societal, and professional ethical standards.

WPI undergraduates complete three major projects that demonstrate their readiness for graduation. The goals of these projects include expectations for inquiry and critical thinking.

### Fostering Achievement of the Goals

WPI's focus on inquiry-based learning centers on three required projects; the first project counts as three credit hours and each of the other two counts as nine credit hours. For the first, the Humanities and Arts Sufficiency, students complete a research or creative project during their first or second year that ties together previous work in a specific area of the humanities or arts. For the second, the Interactive Qualifying Project (IQP), teams of two to four students (usually juniors) address an interdisciplinary problem involving how technology relates to social structures and human needs. The intent is to help students understand how science and technology are embedded in social and cultural contexts. Finally, for the Major Qualifying Project (MQP), teams of two to four seniors complete a research or design project in their major field at a level appropriate to a beginning graduate student or entry-level professional. In this project, students demonstrate that they can apply the appropriate facts, theories, methodologies, and analytic skills of their major area to frame and solve a problem. Depending on the discipline, the focus may be on design, synthesis, experimentation, or theoretical investigation.

Students work on all of these projects in close collaboration with faculty advisers. Most IQPs and MQPs address problems proposed by external agencies or organizations, and all focus on formulating solutions to open-ended, unscripted problems while developing skills in research, teamwork, written and oral communication, and critical thinking. Over 65 percent of WPI students complete at least one of these three projects in a full-time immersion at an off-campus WPI project center; over 50 percent do so at overseas locations, where they live and work as professionals under faculty guidance.

## Assessing the Outcome

All three projects utilize both formative and summative assessments. As students work with their faculty advisers, they receive regular feedback on required elements and progress toward project goals. A formal written report of the students' research and findings is a central outcome of the projects, which often also conclude with an oral presentation either on campus or at the project site. Progress in written, oral, and visual communication is assessed throughout the course of the projects.

For each of the three projects, WPI faculty conduct regular reviews of the written reports for the purposes of programmatic assessment. The scoring of written reports includes three kinds of assessment data: (1) yes/no ratings for the presence or absence of specific report elements; (2) Likert-style ratings for the relative quality of certain elements (such as evidence of specific learning outcomes); and (3) open-ended written comments where the other kinds of ratings are not appropriate. The scoring provides analytical assessment of important elements within each major area, summary scores for each area, and a summary score for the entire report.

The three inquiry-based project requirements are the primary vehicles for assessing students' progress toward campus-wide learning outcomes as well as outcomes for specific majors. WPI offers seven engineering programs accredited by the Accreditation Board for Engineering and Technology (ABET), and the assessment of project reports has played a central role in preparation for ABET visits.

## Improvements Resulting from Assessment Data

Assessment data have contributed to specific changes in all three projects over the past decade. Based on assessments of the Humanities and Arts Sufficiency, WPI faculty recently voted to restructure the overall humanities and arts requirement to ensure more breadth and facilitate team-based work. Assessment of IQP reports has led to significant modifications in the way students are prepared and advised, and has motivated an initiative in writing across the curriculum. Shortcomings detected in reviews of MQPs have prompted faculty to include more open-ended project work and to introduce design activities earlier in core course sequences.

Most significantly, both project assessment data and National Survey of Student Engagement results for first-year students and for juniors and seniors have led to a major initiative to enhance the first year at WPI by introducing project and seminar activities designed to promote critical thinking, develop skills of inquiry, and better prepare students for the project work to come. This initiative represents the first major curriculum revision since WPI adopted its outcomes-oriented projects program in the 1970s.

# Intellectual and Practical Skills

# Teamwork and Problem Solving

## PORTLAND STATE UNIVERSITY (Portland, Oregon)

### Goals

Embedded within Portland State University's general education goal areas of inquiry and critical thinking, communication, and ethics and social responsibility are the expectations that students learn to pose, investigate, and conceptualize problems and collaborate effectively with others in group work.

### Fostering Achievement of the Goals

Portland State's general education program, University Studies, is vertically structured to develop goals across all of the years of a degree program. Experiences fostering teamwork and problem solving begin in the Freshman Inquiry course (FRINQ) and continue each year, culminating with the senior capstone collaborative project.

FRINQ is a yearlong, theme-based course that uses an interdisciplinary and interactive approach to show how topics can be understood from different perspectives. FRINQ classes function as learning communities and include lectures and group dialogue on course content, student-led discussions based on homework assignments, and creative opportunities to challenge and expand thinking. Students collaborate on community-based projects as well as in mentor labs, where they develop and critique e-portfolios that document work related to each of Portland State's four broad learning goals.

Sophomore Inquiry (SINQ) courses introduce students to the concepts, questions, methods, and other content that will be further explored in the subsequent Upper Division Cluster. SINQ courses build on the skills developed in Freshman Inquiry and explore topics of interest that are different from, yet complementary to, students' majors. Graduate mentors who work alongside faculty members guide students through research projects for the course, which often involve community fieldwork in addition to Web and library research.

Upper Division Clusters consist of courses from a variety of disciplines. The courses draw upon the skills and knowledge students have developed in their lower-division University Studies courses. By this time in their academic careers, students are expected to be proficient in writing, research, discussion, and computer and inquiry skills. In Upper Division Cluster courses, students pursue rich, in-depth study of the thematic lines of inquiry introduced in SINQ. Additionally, through their choice of Upper Division Cluster courses, students can design an individualized plan of study based on their academic goals. Many of these courses involve collaborative projects or hands-on community projects.

Senior capstone courses designed by Portland State University's faculty build cooperative learning communities by taking students out of the classroom and into the field. In capstone courses, students apply the knowledge, skills, and interests developed through all aspects of their education to a community project. Students from a variety of majors and backgrounds work as a team, pooling resources and collaborating with faculty and community leaders to understand and find solutions to problems that are important to them as engaged citizens.

### Assessing the Outcome

In addition to in-class assessments of how students work in collaboration (including peer assessments from team members), FRINQ students create course portfolios that document their learning in the four broad goals of University Studies. Faculty members from across the university assess a 20 percent sample of the portfolios using rubrics for each goal area. These data, as well as course surveys, contribute to program assessment.

Student work samples from SINQ and Upper Division Cluster courses are used in a program assessment that cycles through three goal areas per year. In some cases, common assignments among sections provide a more unified look at learning at a particular level.

Several assessment processes generate data on teamwork and problem solving in senior capstone courses. In at least 20 percent of the capstone courses, a trained professional asks students about what has helped them learn, what could be improved, and how to bring about those improvements. Students frequently report that faculty support for working in interdisciplinary groups is beneficial. A faculty development coordinator assists teams of students in learning collaborative skills. In addition, data on effective problem solving based on course evaluations are shared with the faculty. Faculty frequently assign reflective writing assignments (three- to five-page essays) that challenge students to document how they have enhanced critical thinking skills in the capstone's collaborative context. Pilot studies are underway to begin evaluation of student work samples.

Portland State has also developed detailed protocols to guide the use of assessment data within the University Studies program, making very clear what may be shared and for what purposes. Such clarity in the use of data, particularly regarding assessment of faculty work, helps to create a culture in which assessment is valued and used to improve student learning.

### Improvements Resulting from Assessment Data

Direct assessment of student work, from FRINQ portfolios to capstone projects, improves all levels of University Studies. Assessment data have resulted in changes in course themes, texts, assignments, and pedagogies. Portland State has also used data to identify particular outcome areas for faculty development, including collaboration and problem solving.

Mid-quarter and end-of-term capstone evaluations help determine whether each capstone fosters effective problem-solving skills. A faculty development coordinator dedicated to working with capstone faculty helps resolve capstone-specific issues and respond to student feedback. For example, students' comments resulted in better delineation of the structure of collaborative projects and improved clarity in specific grading criteria for complex collaborative courses.

# Personal and Social Responsibility

# Civic Engagement

## WAGNER COLLEGE (Staten Island, New York)

### Goals

Wagner College's goals for civic engagement are related to its commitment to experiential learning. Wagner prepares students to be reflective practitioners within their chosen professions and to be socially conscious in their personal and professional lives.

### Fostering Achievement of the Goals

Wagner requires all students to complete three levels of learning communities (during the first year, the middle two years, and the senior year), with the first and third levels requiring experiential learning. The intermediate learning community focuses on improving student writing proficiency but may include a field experience or study abroad.

Taught by full-time faculty, first-year learning communities consist of two courses, a "reflective tutorial," and at least thirty hours of experiential learning related to the theme of the learning community. Recent learning communities have included "The Wheel of Fortune," which paired courses in politics and macroeconomics, and "Creativity and Conflict in Modern Times," which focused on the study of modern art and modern Western civilization. With student placements available across greater New York City, the possibilities for connecting students' academic work to experiential learning off campus are plentiful. In the reflective tutorial, students explore the connections among classroom and field experiences through written assignments and analytical discussions.

Intermediate learning communities address interdisciplinary topics that allow students to see the social and intellectual connections among diverse perspectives. While direct civic participation is not required, emphasis on social aspects of the disciplines keeps students' civic awareness high during the middle years of their programs.

The Senior Program, Wagner's third learning community, combines a capstone course in the major, an experiential component (such as a field-based practicum or applied project involving original research), and a reflective tutorial. The reflective tutorial brings together students within a major to discuss their experiences, share findings and research techniques, and integrate learning across their entire degree program. Reengagement with off-campus learning during the senior year prepares students to leave campus upon graduation with deep knowledge and understanding of how their learning can be used for the benefit of communities.

A new curricular option, the "certificate of civic engagement," is available for students wishing to increase their commitment to community service and off-campus learning. In addition to the normal learning community requirements, certificate students study domestic poverty, take a course with an international focus or study abroad, and complete additional community service for a total of 270 hours.

## Assessing the Outcome

Assessment of civic engagement takes many forms at Wagner. Especially important to the first-year program are monthly meetings of the faculty to discuss what is working and what is not. There are ongoing discussions to improve the matching of a community placement with an academic course. A first-year program review committee analyzes course proposals to ensure that they meet program standards and also monitors current offerings for continued appropriateness.

A short, student-completed survey gives faculty insight into first-year students' perceptions of the learning outcomes and of the value of their placements. Site supervisor surveys confirm student attendance and basic participation. These processes provide sufficient assessment of first-year students' participation in the community.

Direct assessments of student learning come from journals that students keep, writing and other assignments, and especially the senior capstone projects. Discussions during first-year and senior reflective tutorials convey additional rich information about students' civic experiences and learning.

## Improvements Resulting from Assessment Data

Many improvements have resulted from the ongoing assessment of civic engagement at Wagner College. Basic improvements, like college-provided transportation to community sites and better understanding of which students will match the various placements, have resulted from discussions and surveys.

The college has offered faculty development to address concerns arising from the surveys. Two-day faculty retreats foster improved writing instruction and assignment planning, and have resulted in changes to both content and the quantity of assignments.

Wagner has designated a faculty coordinator to help ensure quality in the first-year and senior programs. Additionally, a guidebook for faculty based upon data from assessments explains minimum standards for important elements of the program.

Finally, faculty innovations and grant funding are creating new ways for students to become civically engaged. To meet needs revealed by both formal and informal assessments, some faculty are locating and shaping community programs to engage students with specific interests—for example, through a first-year project in biology at a "Superfund" site. To address a perceived need for increasing the developmental and cumulative outcomes of civic engagement, Wagner sought and received grant funding to plan new departmental and curricular connections. Two departments have been linked with specific community agencies; each department has developed four courses in its curriculum that have a service-learning component and require students to participate actively in the community agency's work. Now only in its first year, this new effort is already being assessed, and it will be expanded from two to six departments over the next three years.

# Personal and Social Responsibility

# Ethical Practice

## UNIVERSITY OF CHARLESTON (Charleston, West Virginia)

### Goals

Members of the campus community at the University of Charleston (UC) embrace and seek to apply core ethical values to all aspects of their living, working, and learning at the university as well as to their personal lives in the wider community. These values include justice, integrity, respect, responsibility, and altruism. The university has established specific ethical practice learning outcomes for all students.

Ethical practice requires that each student
- understands, articulates, and demonstrates the core values of the university community—justice, integrity, respect, responsibility, and altruism;
- identifies and resolves moral conflicts;
- demonstrates ability to make and implement informed and responsible ethical decisions.

### Fostering Achievement of the Goals

UC students learn about ethical practice at foundational, intermediate, and advanced levels of the curriculum through a series of planned activities that constitute a "developmental approach" to achieving the outcomes.

During orientation, activities designed by student life staff with the assistance of peer educators introduce new students to the university's mission and core values. Students also take the Defining Issues Test (DIT), which assesses their level of moral development. Advisers use the results later in the first year.

At the foundational level (during the first year), students complete one-credit-hour courses in both the fall and spring semesters taught by a faculty mentor and a peer educator. These courses introduce students to the university and its curriculum. Students complete assignments for the courses that demonstrate communication and ethical practice competencies. The fall course reinforces core values through exploration of relationships among university regulations, such as academic integrity and residence life policies. The spring course introduces students to ethical practice through specific assignments. Faculty score these assignments using a university-wide rubric—the Ethical Practice and Decision-Making Assessment Scale—and students compile the assignments in a portfolio. Faculty members also talk individually with first-year students about the implications of their DIT score for choosing courses.

At the intermediate level (during the sophomore and junior years), students continue ethical development while taking two designated courses that provide intensive experience with ethical practice. Experiences may consist of written and oral presentations as well as group discussions that faculty evaluate with the same rubric used in the first year. The university also encourages all students to participate in cocurricular activities (including forums, film series, and community services) to explore ethical dimensions of personal, professional, and civic life.

At the advanced level (in the senior year), capstone experiences in and out of the major provide opportunities to exercise ethical decision making and personal accountability. Faculty evaluation, as well as students' own reflections on their development of ethical practice and decision making (based upon evidence in their portfolio), are used to assess achievement of graduation-level competency. Graduation-level competency is defined, in part, as a score of 3 or 4 on work assessed with the Ethical Practice and Decision-Making Assessment Scale.

## Assessing the Outcome

Assessments within courses are used formatively to improve future student learning of ethical practice. The close relationship among students, peer mentors, and advisers during several early experiences in ethical development make such formative assessment possible and effective. An electronic portfolio archives student work related to liberal learning outcomes and provides faculty and students a mechanism for tracking progress of learning in the outcomes.

UC is positioned to begin using the electronic portfolios to conduct program and institution-level assessments of liberal learning outcomes, including ethical practice. Faculty committees or "roundtables" take responsibility for assessing the university's achievement of its stated learning outcomes. The use of a uniform rubric across ethical practice experiences, from entry to graduation, assists with this assessment.

## Improvements Resulting from Assessment Data

Each roundtable works with the curriculum committee to ensure that there are sufficient opportunities for students to learn and to demonstrate their capabilities in each liberal education outcome. Roundtable members regularly review course descriptions and assignments to ensure that the outcome is being addressed across the university's offerings. The roundtable also assists with faculty development for fostering the outcomes.

As more data become available from the analysis of student learning portfolios, the roundtables will include those data in their recommendations for revision and development of curricular offerings.

Personal and Social Responsibility

# Intercultural Knowledge and Competence

## DRURY UNIVERSITY (Springfield, Missouri)

### Goals

The required Global Perspectives 21 curriculum (GP 21) prepares all students at Drury University for living in an ever-changing global society. Because global issues are infused across the general education curriculum, general education goals are also GP 21 goals.

The following GP 21 goals explicitly refer to global issues:
- Prepare students for leadership roles. . . . Students will gain experience in integrating multiple experiences and diverse sources of information into innovative solutions to contemporary issues—both local and global.
- Develop student understanding of the Western tradition, scientific and quantitative reasoning, and the diversity of human experiences and cultures.
- Foster cross-cultural understanding, recognizing the value and integrity of multiple world cultures, religions, etc., and skill in cross-cultural communication that rests upon mutual respect and understanding.

The following GP 21 outcomes explicitly refer to global issues:
- Graduates will apply disciplinary, multidisciplinary, and interdisciplinary models of analysis to contemporary world issues.
- Graduates will demonstrate an understanding of globalization's causes and effects.
- Graduates will be able to identify and explain significant ideas and events of Western culture, including key elements of the American experience.
- Graduates will be able to analyze diverse traditions, social institutions, and symbolic systems.

All Drury students graduate with a minor in global studies as a result of the GP 21 curriculum.

### Fostering Achievement of the Goals

Four required global studies courses create a "spine" across programs so that students revisit and develop global studies outcomes as they progress through their first three years. In addition to global studies, students take required and elective disciplinary studies courses that develop multiple liberal education outcomes while often considering global issues or contexts.

Within the sixty to sixty-nine course credit hours that comprise the full GP 21 curriculum, students
- study the American experience, with an emphasis on minority communities;
- select a foreign language for at least a year of study;
- develop global awareness and learn about cultural diversity;
- use science and inquiry to explore world issues;

- learn about both traditional Western and nontraditional values and value systems;
- imagine the future by reviewing theoretical approaches to globalization, examining current events, and considering how the great ideas of the past might be applied to contemporary issues and challenges;
- complete an integrative senior project in their major;
- select among elective courses that enrich global understanding.

### Assessing the Outcome

Rather than creating independent assessments for each of its goals, Drury primarily uses existing assessment practices. Over the past decade, university assessment teams have assessed writing samples from global studies courses and research papers from department-based senior seminars to gather data on several outcomes, including understanding of concepts in Western thought, globalization, and global issues.

The data reveal that students engage in interdisciplinary thinking only if faculty provide clear models and focused writing and research prompts. The data also indicate that, to develop these skills, faculty should cover less material but engage it more deeply and from multiple viewpoints. Students cannot learn about globalization in a piecemeal fashion in courses with other main objectives. Key Western concepts, such as capitalism, democracy, and human rights, can connect traditional definitions of liberal learning with today's focus on globalization. The data show as well that department-based senior seminars, because they emphasize professional development, are not always the best forums for emphasizing global issues. Finally, most faculty still need to be trained to think in interdisciplinary ways and encouraged to join the many national conversations on this topic.

In 2005, Drury created a forty-five-question global knowledge test that students take during their first week of college and again at the conclusion of their junior year. Two administrations of the test have shown a modest increase in global knowledge, although faculty comments and graduating senior focus groups have indicated that the test does not fully capture what students have learned. The early results also suggest that global learning is more about thought processes than knowledge acquisition, that student growth is most pronounced in the application of geographical and cultural knowledge, and that multiple-choice instruments are fairly limited as tools for measuring global learning.

### Improvements Resulting from Assessment Data

Drury University has made a number of changes based upon findings from assessments and surveys. The course on global awareness and cultural diversity now covers fewer cultures but explores them in far more detail, emphasizing the study of culture more deeply. Some faculty have begun asking students to research and write about more specific topics, and more detailed research projects have resulted in better writing, improved critical thinking, and greater cultural awareness. A global awareness reader now brings together classic readings on cultural analysis, which is taught in all sections of the required Global Awareness and Cultural Diversity course. Another required course, Global Futures, now emphasizes the study of globalization and transnationalism, and faculty have transformed the second half of the course into a research seminar. By including global learning within college assessment protocols, Drury has also created a number of forums for faculty to discuss and reflect upon how better to engage global learning.

**Personal and Social Responsibility**

# Foundation and Skills for Lifelong Learning

## SAN JOSÉ STATE UNIVERSITY (San José, California)

### Goals

The mission statements of many colleges and universities express the expectation that graduates will be lifelong learners. Unfortunately, a thorough investigation of lifelong learning logically requires repeated assessments of alumni from graduation onward. Additionally, even if post-graduation measures were to show continued learning, it would be difficult to establish a causal relationship between college attendance and continuing ability and willingness to learn—many other factors may intervene.

The Accreditation Board for Engineering and Technology (ABET), the accreditor for engineering programs, requires that engineering programs "demonstrate that their graduates have… a recognition of the need for, and an ability to engage in lifelong learning" (www.abet.org). By asking for evidence of *preparation* for lifelong learning, ABET places the learning and assessment focus on actions *during*, not after, college, thus suggesting that a multiyear effort during the degree program is needed to foster and assess this important area of liberal education.

Through an analysis of the engineering curriculum and a consideration of which courses aligned most closely with ABET-required outcomes, the engineering department at San José State University chose several specific courses in which to monitor the development and assessment of preparation for lifelong learning. Nikos Mourtos, professor of engineering at San José State, suggests that preparation for lifelong learning should be developed by close attention to both "affective" and "cognitive" elements—the affective elements related to "recognition of need for" lifelong learning and the cognitive elements to the "ability to engage" (see fie.engrng.pitt.edu/fie2003/papers/1367.pdf). Referring to the taxonomy of the affective domain, Mourtos asserts that students should be at or above the "organization" level to meet the ABET standard (the five levels of the taxonomy include receiving, responding, valuing, organization, and characterization). Mourtos defines organization as the ability to balance responsibilities effectively and to begin to formulate a systematic approach to learning. For the cognitive domain, students are expected to be at the "analysis" level or higher (from among the six levels of knowledge, comprehension, application, analysis, synthesis, and evaluation).

### Fostering Achievement of the Goals

To develop affective outcomes, engineering students at San José State talk with representatives from professional societies, discuss reasons for pursuing a graduate degree, and complete learning style inventories. The first two activities represent a conscious effort to shape students' attitudes toward postcollege learning while they are in the program. Data from the learning style inventories show students' strengths and weaknesses in learning and guide efforts to overcome weaknesses and balance individual learning approaches.

Course assignments and projects—beginning with reverse engineering and mathematical modeling projects in an introductory engineering course and continuing in subsequent courses with problem solving, design, and design improvement—develop cognitive outcomes.

## Assessing the Outcome

The department's three-part assessment process includes analysis of student work, student course reflections, and student surveys. Student actions indicative of at least the "organization" level of affect include willingness to learn new material on one's own; reflecting on the learning process; participating in professional societies' activities; reading engineering articles and books outside of class; and attending extracurricular training or planning to attend graduate school.

Evidence confirming cognitive capabilities include reading critically and assessing the quality of information available; synthesizing new concepts by making connections, transferring prior knowledge, and generalizing; analyzing new content by breaking it down, asking key questions, comparing and contrasting, recognizing patterns, and interpreting information; and reasoning by predicting, inferring, using inductions, questioning assumptions, using lateral thinking, and inquiring.

## Improvements Resulting from Assessment Data

The engineering department selects a faculty member as a "champion" for a particular outcome and that person recommends curricular and other changes needed to improve student achievement of the outcome. Data from assessments have raised questions about whether the department's expectations for assessment results need to be revised and whether the right assignments have been chosen to assess the affective elements of the outcome. When data indicate a need for improvement, the department examines factors such as course design, instructor effectiveness, and student abilities and motivation.

# Integration and Synthesis across General and Specialized Studies

## HAMPSHIRE COLLEGE (Amherst, Massachusetts)

### Goals

Hampshire College students qualify for the bachelor of arts degree by completing a full-time program composed of three divisions of study with the aim of accomplishing specific learning objectives. Although not mentioned explicitly among the objectives, integrative thinking and learning are closely associated with the following six program goals:

- Engage in critical analysis
- Learn to express ideas in a range of modes and media
- Develop the imagination
- Contextualize the making of art in a broader theoretical context
- Develop historical, multicultural, political, social, and cultural perspectives on academic work
- Engage in self-initiated work for which the student feels ownership

The three divisions of the curriculum are intentionally structured to ensure that students develop as integrative thinkers and learners throughout their time at Hampshire.

### Fostering Achievement of the Goals

In Division I, students pursue foundational studies in the liberal arts by designing their own first-year curriculum guided by a flexible distribution requirement. As students progress through Division I, they prepare a portfolio that includes course evaluations, samples of their work, and a reflective, integrative self-evaluation of their studies. Integration is supported throughout Division I studies by student self-evaluations written for each course taken and by formative assessments of the portfolio as it develops.

In Division II, students explore their chosen field(s) of emphasis through an individually designed program of courses, independent work, and internships or field studies. Each student's creation of a coherent plan of study is itself integrative, and this plan is enriched by other integrative experiences: a multicultural perspective requirement, studies outside the concentration, and community service that is expected to be relevant to the area of concentration. From planning a concentration to selecting work that provides evidence of having satisfactorily completed the concentration, students must actively integrate their learning. At the end of the concentration (typically, four semesters of work), students submit a Division II portfolio.

The formal portfolio review and a required retrospective essay foster continuing integration. A two-person faculty committee considers each student's work longitudinally and as a whole. These faculty work together with the student to find patterns in the work, point out and deepen the appreciation of connections, identify strengths, and address weaknesses.

In Division III—Advanced Studies—students complete a major independent study project centered on a specific topic, question, or idea. The Division III project—whether a thesis, portfolio, film, exhibit, recital, or performance, or a committee-approved combination of these—is evaluated by the faculty committee that approved the project. Such projects elicit high-level integration of students' cumulative learning. In addition to the independent project, students complete two advanced educational activities (taking courses, co-teaching a college course, or completing an internship or independent study) that often provide additional integrative emphasis.

Hampshire has a strong commitment to interdisciplinarity. There are no departments and no majors. Students must propose their own Division II concentration and Division III yearlong independent project. Hence, students are expected to identify their questions, to chart out a coherent curriculum (based on those questions), and to reflect, review, and modify their course of study as the work unfolds. All of this promotes ownership of the curriculum and exploration of the connections among the strands of the work.

### Assessing the Outcome

Assessment of the outcome takes place through evaluation of the division portfolios and the independent study project. These "division-embedded" direct assessments of student work provide rich information about students' progress toward Hampshire's learning goals and their integrative thinking and learning. Students' regular self-assessments infuse reflective and integrative opportunities across the curriculum, stimulating integrative growth, synthesis, and development.

### Improvements Resulting from Assessment Data

Because Hampshire's assessment of the transition from Division I to Division II indicated that for many students, the concentration tended to be too compressed, the college has recently expanded the Division II expectation from three semesters to four semesters of work. This change in the requirements for Division II promotes greater integration of student learning in the concentration by encouraging students to engage in a richer course of study and a prolonged period of scholarly reflection. The expanded Division II also permits more substantial preparation for the yearlong independent study project in Division III.

Hampshire's Educational Policy Committee recently completed a study of Division II that focused on determining the characteristics of the most successful concentrations. As a result of this assessment, one of the new interdisciplinary programs at the college—the Foundation for Psychocultural Research–Hampshire College Program in Culture, Brain, and Development—adopted a matrix for students to use when developing their concentrations. The program now asks students to build concentrations that reflect three qualities: *intellectual breadth*, *core studies*, and *integration*. This is the first time that "integration" has been identified as an independent learning goal at Hampshire; the college expects this formalization not only to strengthen Division II but also to contribute to its longstanding goal of promoting intentional learning.

# References

Association of American Colleges and Universities. 2002. *Greater expectations: A new vision for learning as a nation goes to college.* Washington, DC: Association of American Colleges and Universities.

———. 2004a. *Our students' best work: A framework for accountability worthy of our mission.* Washington, DC: Association of American Colleges and Universities.

———. 2004b. *Taking responsibility for the quality of the baccalaureate degree.* Washington, DC: Association of American Colleges and Universities.

———. 2005. *Liberal education outcomes: A preliminary report on student achievement in college.* Washington, DC: Association of American Colleges and Universities.

———. 2007. *College learning for the new global century: A report from the National Leadership Council for Liberal Education and America's Promise.* Washington, DC: Association of American Colleges and Universities.

Shavelson, R. J. 2007. *A brief history of student learning assessment: How we got where we are and a proposal for where to go next.* Washington, DC: Association of American Colleges and Universities.

# About the Author

**Ross Miller** is director of programs for the Office of Quality, Curriculum, and Assessment at AAC&U. He holds a BM and MM in trumpet performance from the University of Michigan and an EdD in music education from the University of Illinois.

Miller came to AAC&U at the start of the Greater Expectations initiative and has contributed extensively to project meetings and publications since 1999. As a faculty member and as the assistant director of the AAC&U Institute on General Education, he has focused on the teaching/learning cycle and direct assessment of student learning, especially formative assessment.

During his thirteen years at Nazareth College in Rochester, New York, Miller worked with the undergraduate music education program and subsequently was appointed the first director of the graduate program in music education. Additionally, he taught applied trumpet and all levels of music education, directed the college band, and supervised student teachers. He was president of the Council of Music Teacher Education Programs, an affiliate of the New York State School Music Association (NYSSMA).

In an assignment as assessment coordinator for Nazareth College, Miller was responsible for assessment of the college's general education program. An early advocate of portfolio assessment, he has presented at regional and national music educators conventions. He was invited to serve as a question writer in the arts for the National Assessment of Educational Progress and to work on the NYSSMA team developing a high school outcomes test in the arts for the New York State Education Department.